HE SPOKE

A MEMOIR OF GRACE

HE SPOKE

A MEMOIR OF GRACE

DIANA LÉGERE

Arabelle Publishing, LLC
Chesterfield, Virginia

He Spoke: A Memoir of Grace
© 2022 by Diana Lé Gere

Published by Arabelle Publishing, LLC.
www.arabellebooks.com
Instagram: @arabellepublishing and @arabellebooks
Submit inquires through our website.

These stories reveal the author's memory of events. Some of the character names have been changed to safeguard the privacy of the individuals. It is nearly impossible to recall a conversation exactly. The dialogue in this story is not meant to be a word-for-word, but an inspired account based on the original experiences that took place in the author's life. These stories portray the author's memory and feelings as she journeys through a trek backward in time.

Scripture is taken from the King James Version unless otherwise cited.

ISBN (978-0-9979126-1-6)
First edition 10 9 8 7 6 5 4 3 2 1
Printed in the USA

To Amanda

May you always see the blessings God has woven into your life. In tough times, look back on these stories and remember the hand of God, and trust in the Lord to see you through whatever lies ahead as you walk along your journey. God is a light to your path and a lamp to your feet.

"And thine ears shall hear a word behind thee, saying This Way, walk ye in it, when ye turn to the right hand and when ye turn to the left."

Isaiah 30:21

CONTENTS

ACKNOWLEDGMENTS

I am blessed to have had the joy of meeting God's ambassadors, who have supported and encouraged me spiritually and emotionally during trying times. These people have spoken words of life and blessing over me and my children. Genuine believers who never wavered and set an example for me by witnessing their lives and showing me a genuine commitment to Jesus in their walk and talk.

INTRODUCTION

God's will for us (if we are brave enough to accept His gift) is to rest in Him so He can move in and through our lives. We need not *do* anything or try to *be* anything, for God already knows us. He loves us as we are and right where we are. He can transform us and use us mightily if we let Him.

Fearfully and wonderfully made, He has carved a unique foundation to cradle our hearts and soul. He alone knows the outcome of our individual journey. Trust in Him. When a situation seems impossible for man, God can do far more than we can ever imagine.

This book is a collection of memories of special times that God spoke to me. Not audibly, but an impression on my heart or through people and circumstances. I'm embarrassed to say, too many times I wasn't paying attention. Sometimes I heard Him but refused to listen. But each time I stepped out in faith and obeyed His call, He met me with blessings.

These experiences helped build my faith and allow me (now) to recognize his voice more clearly. It's a voice of soothing grace. Take a journey with me. As you read my stories, I hope you may even recall a few precious moments of your own.

Invite God's presence to shine into your soul, and amazing things will happen. Your heart will expand to receive the love letters He's written just for you.

Take note as God speaks to you, and the gentle waves of His voice will give you peace beyond any human understanding. Prepare to receive His timely messages, and when He speaks, you will know without a doubt you're headed in the right direction.

By the Word of the Lord, the heavens were made,
And all the host of them by the breath of His mouth.
He gathers the waters of the sea together as a heap.
He lays the deep in storehouses.
Let all the earth fear the Lord.
Let all the inhabitants of the world stand in awe of Him
for He Spoke, and it was done.

Psalm 33:6-9

CHAPTER 1

I Never Promised You a Joyride

A sudden jolt and pellets of glass hitting the dashboard got my full attention. Moments before, we reveled in a leisurely drive on a beautiful, sunny day. It was a familiar country drive. Only this trip started differently and ended worse than I ever imagined.

Have you ever felt a tight piercing in the pit of your stomach? You're enjoying a moment, and then it hits you. An undeniable sense that something is wrong. You've done or said something WRONG. That afternoon, my stomach churned and twisted with incessant internal warnings.

"Your dad will never know!" My friend pushed me, but I stood firm. Or at least, it was my plan.

"Nope. I can't. Dad said drive there and back. NO joy rides."

"It's not a joyride," she persisted. "It's a little ride down the road. Come on, I've never ridden in a jeep before." Before I could respond, she hopped in the passenger seat.

Sue was still a senior in high school; I had graduated the year before. I lived the facade of a confident "grown-up" life with a paying job, yet she had more guts and confidence as a teenager. She got what she wanted. Every time. And if she wanted me to do something, I'd be doing it.

My conscience was stretching as if it would tear in half. The good girl in me wanted to stay true to my dad, but the devil taunted me to give in to my friend's wishes. *What kind of best friend was I, anyway?* She asked for a quick ride. Would a 10-minute jaunt around the corner be *that* bad?

I agreed half-heartedly. But who was I kidding? It wouldn't do any good to ask her to get out, especially if I really would refuse her a ride. She'd sit in protest until I started the engine.

No matter how I tried to justify it, it was wrong. Nothing seemed right about this. Dad gave me permission to drive the jeep to work and back home. Nothing more. No shopping. And definitely no leisure drives. License to travel to a friend's house was a huge exception. Particularly a friend who lived on a snake country road with no speed limits.

God had spoken to my spirit. His voice was a subtle tap, but felt by my heart. Too polite to demand. A simple nudge, "Don't go, my child." I wanted to listen, really I did. But, I needed to make my friend happy, too.

Bathed in shattered glass, I watched the last moments flash through my mind like a movie in super-speed rewind mode. Voices bellowed in my head, "HOW DID YOU LET THIS HAPPEN?" In one second, a wrong decision shifted the course of several lives.

As blood trickled down Sue's forehead, I noticed the smashed windshield and the hole where her face struck the glass.

Even then, I wasn't listening to my friend or God. And I wasn't a tiny bit intimidated by the gray-haired lady screaming at me through the driver's window, demanding that someone buy her a new mailbox.

My selfishness got the best of me. All I thought of was the full tank of gas I traded for a fist full of cash. Money wasted, like spending an entire day at school but being marked absent, anyway. Plus, a good chunk of my hard-earned paycheck was gone, and I'd wait a week for another one. Worst of all, I had no transportation.

I huffed and pounded the steering wheel. "We need to move this jeep." Although silent to the world, in my head, I'm screaming at her, *why aren't you helping me?!* I wanted to shake some sense into her.

She lifted her head and glared at me as if I had said it out loud. Her icy stare told me I was out of my mind. And at that minute, I was.

"*Where* do you think we should move it?" Her sarcasm hit me like a dodge ball.

Illogical thinking, but all I wanted to do was park the smashed jeep with a full tank of gas in my father's driveway. In my state of delusion, it would have made more sense than calling him to pull me out of a demolished pile of metal still smoldering and hissing.

I turned the key. Nothing. I got out and inspected the vehicle. Two wheels had dislodged. The smashed front end looked like an accordion buried deep into the hundred-year-old tree trunk. Through the grace of God, I stood without a scrape, but my friend had just gone through the windshield.

My father trusted me, and I let him down. This jeep was his pride and joy. The echo of my father's voice kept repeating, firm and clear... *there and back... there and back.*

"I promise. There and back," I said, dancing my way to the jeep while waving the Peter Frampton album I planned to return to my friend. *I couldn't believe it! Driving for fun. Life was good.*

It never dawned on me that after I had made the poor judgment of taking this quick ride, turn after the turn, I unwittingly headed in the wrong direction. En route, my internal navigator kicked in, and He spoke again.

I heard the tiny voice deep in my spirit. *"Go back."* I froze. Turning left would have led straight to her driveway. About the time we could have already grabbed a coke and danced to Peter Frampton, Sue snapped me out of my stupor. "Turn right!" Then I heard it again, *"Go back."* A mental game of tug of war. My friend won.

I'll never forget hearing God's warning before the crash. Not an audible sound, but a sense of knowing He had a personal message for me. A word I ignored.

It happened so fast. Seconds later, I never even felt the impact. The wrecked vehicle was evidence we should have died in that crash. But God had a plan. It took days before my muscles felt the full force of that collision. I drifted through the week like a beaten rag doll, hardly moving to avoid pain. My muscles were stiff, my body ached. I felt like a toy soldier running on a weak battery.

I paid hefty consequences that day. We think we are on a beautiful ride when we are in control, doing it our way. But we discover that unless we're in the palm of God's hand, we do not understand where the road leads until it's too late. Whenever God is not involved from the start, no matter how good it looks, you're left with ashes.

I've learned that if I take time to be still, I can hear Him guiding me and directing me to the right road. Sometimes it's a peaceful feeling. Other times, a word drops into my spirit. In His perfect timing, He will speak to all of us. The question is, will we listen?

He Speaks to Protect Us

We will never know all the ways God protects us as we go about our busy days. Missed turns, delays, and canceled appointments may all be part of His divine plan to direct and redirect our path to keep us safe from harm.

I remember as a first-time mom; the safety of my precious baby girl was an obsession. So much so that I refused to take her out of the house. Thinking back, I'm sure we may have stayed there until she reached school age if I'd gotten my way, but a well-meaning best friend assured me I was overly protective. So much she coerced me into taking my 2-week-old to the mall. The first problem, I had to give up control. She was driving. Second, all I could think of was chaos, screaming kids running around, gangsters, and germs. Somebody might get hurt. What if she got lost? And at the very least, people would tell me how cute she was and might want to get a close look. What if they tried to touch her? Now that would have been entirely off-limits. And I couldn't imagine how I'd keep her warm. It was February.

This tiny baby depended on me for everything. Her dark eyes and sweet smile mesmerized me as she lay in my arms. I was in love in a way I couldn't define and had never felt before. This was my offspring, and I wanted to do everything in my power to protect her from danger. I had baby-proofed the house but had no clue how to baby-proof the world. Scared half to death, I layered and bundled her to ward off the enemy and ventured off to lead the first field trip of my baby's life.

God is like that with us. He protects us from danger. Only instead of wrapping us in layers, He becomes a shield to guard us against enemy attacks. The psalmist says, our soul waits for the Lord; He is our help and our protection. God is with us whenever we need help. We need no appointment. We are to come to Him boldly. "Let us, therefore, come boldly to the throne of grace, that we may obtain mercy and find grace to help in time of need" (Hebrews 4:16 NKJV).

Back to this first trip. I think it's ironic that it would end in a police car. The plan was that my husband would pick us up at the mall later that evening. The problem was that he drove a vehicle with expired tags. And in New York, that meant more than a simple ticket. Our car was impounded. What were the chances of our expired tags being noticed in the dark? This day, 100%. A capable and robust police officer would escort us to the station, where we could make a call to get a safe ride home. And through it all, my little bundle of joy slept safely in her parent's care, knowing our shield was protecting her from danger just as my father is careful to protect me.

"But the Lord is faithful.
He will establish you and guard you against the evil one."

2 Thessalonians 3:3

Prayer

Father, thank You for speaking. You promised to be our guide even unto death. I trust you will instruct me and teach me, but sometimes I need help to listen. My heart wants to go one way, yet You direct my steps toward a better way. I give You this day. Be the lamp to my feet and the light to my path.

In Jesus' name. Amen.

REFLECTION

Recall a time you thought you heard God instructing you in a situation. What happened, and how did you respond?

_____

_____

_____

_____

_____

_____

_____

What temptations have you encountered? Describe your obedience or disobedience.

_____

_____

_____

_____

_____

_____

_____

_____

HE SPOKE

Describe the ways God speaks to you in your situations?

_____

_____

_____

_____

_____

_____

_____

_____

Have you ever encountered a situation when you were protected from danger, and you knew it was the hand of God?

_____

_____

_____

_____

_____

_____

_____

_____

_____

_____

JOURNAL YOUR STORY

_____

_____

_____

_____

_____

_____

_____

_____

_____

_____

_____

_____

_____

_____

_____

_____

_____

_____

_____

_____

_____

_____

HE SPOKE

CHAPTER 2

Trading Houses

'That's crazy! You're abandoning everything in your life to move 2,000 miles across the country?"

All my friends spurted a similar reaction to this news, and I was getting impatient with repeating myself. Recording an answer sounded better each day.

"It's such a great opportunity," I'd tell them. An adventure. But they were right. It made little sense. I had started a photography business only months before and loved every minute. I had several customers contracted for the fall. It committed me.

New York held the foundation of our hearts and soul. We loved the city. Our friends were like family, and we had an active social life. This place is we had collected all our memories through laughter and tears. We were close to our families and enjoyed taking our toddlers on evening stroller rides to visit their grandparents. Why would we move?

Because my sister-in-law blurted it out during a 4th of July family picnic. "You should move to Utah," she said, talking through her grilled burger.

17

Did I hear her right? I found little in common with Utah. And logic told me no one in their right mind moved to Utah. It was where the cowboys lived.

I had never been to the west, except on a bus trip I took with my mom to California. We took a three-week vacation to visit my sister in Santa Maria after she joined the Air Force. I loved the Pacific coast and came back with a heart's desire to move to the sunshine state. But the gap between my love of beaches and desert was far and wide. Utah seemed a little outside of America.

Lynn moved to Utah in the early 60s with her husband and a dog named Maxwell. Ready to take on the wild west adventure, they packed their belongings into a hippie Volkswagen van, headed west, and never looked back.

Twenty years later, she had built a beautiful life in a lovely neighborhood along the Wasatch mountains.

"It's a terrific place to raise a family," she said. "Excellent schools, healthy living, and mountains. It's beautiful. So much to do."

I loved the mountains. But we had them in New York. Lots of them—the Adirondacks and the Catskills. We needed more than mountains to entice us to leave. Mark took even longer to convince. "Really, Utah?" Although he had visited twice, at first, she didn't sell him on the idea.

I'm not sure what motivated her to invite us. But the timely message resonated with my spirit—we were called. After some persuasion, we both agreed; sight unseen, we prepared to move our family to Utah.

I love my family, and leaving any of them required a lot of soul-searching. This move made no sense. I had a good rapport with my mom and cherished our coffee chats and lunch dates. My kids loved their "special grandma."

I devoted Sunday afternoons to visiting my grandmother, who also loved my children with all her heart and soul.

These were her only great-grandchildren. They brought her joy, and our weekly visits gave her something to live for. Leaving her and my mother meant giving up two lifeline relationships.

Moving away from everything—family, friends, my job, and all we were accustomed to—wasn't anywhere on my radar. And not on my husband's radar because we lived only blocks from the house he grew up in. We enjoyed spending frequent visits with his four brothers. Utah would mean not only a change of scenery but new customs and a complete lifestyle shift. Although not known, leaving New York would be a culture shock!

Yet one month later, we stocked up on strapping tape and collected boxes. I never planned to get rid of anything important, but we had to make sacrifices. We made hard choices and said goodbye to a few favorite things, with the winners neatly packed inside 102 boxes shipped by UPS. That was it. Our life was in boxes, and we stood by, waiting for the day we would board a plane to meet our new life in Utah. Meanwhile, Lynn offered to gather and keep everything safe until we would arrive in the fall.

Although I didn't see how this would pan out or where we would live, I believed we were supposed to move. We held a garage sale and sold everything we didn't need. Bigger things we couldn't sell, we left in the house for my mom and her husband, who would sublet our flat.

Designed by an expert planner, everything seemed to slide into place. We bought one-way plane tickets for next to nothing. Lynn called to tell us she found a cute home on a treelined street for only $350 a month with no deposit required. And it was less than we were paying in rent.

At 6 a.m., only days after my son's first birthday, we were ready to leave. My mom must have been heartbroken to see her grandkids move. But she never criticized our decision or made me feel guilty. Armed with only two suitcases, we said our last goodbyes and hugged until time ran out.

We loaded up in the vehicle, and with our toddlers and a couple of suitcases, we embarked on a blind journey to our future. My father-in-law drove us to LaGuardia. In two hours, we'd be boarding a plane, never to look back at the familiar home that held our hearts. Tonight, I would cook dinner in a new house we had never seen before.

The flight was smooth, both of us absorbed in thoughts of what this change meant. I leaned out the window, allowing my body to unite with the exhaustion and hope of what lay ahead.

By late afternoon, we arrived in Salt Lake City. As we descended for a landing, I couldn't believe my eyes. I saw the brightest blue sky I had ever seen. Amidst this backdrop, a beautiful metropolitan city cradled by massive mountains. Mountains so colossal they looked as if they could swallow the entire town. This place made the Adirondack and Catskill mountains of upstate New York look like tiny hills. I was in awe. Something came alive in me. We were in for something bigger than we imagined. I was so excited to explore this city. If this was the desert, I loved it!

Lynn and Tom got us at the airport. The ride home gave us a peek of beautiful treelined streets with immaculate yards. This place was like a postcard, picture-perfect and pristine. Nothing like we had back home. Super plush green lawns. Not a speck of trash lay strewn alongside any street we drove. From the airport to the house, we saw not a soda can or a cigarette butt, or anything remotely misplaced. A road so peaceful, it was as we had stepped onto a movie set. *Could a neighborhood be this flawless?*

We were surprised and overjoyed that our new home was move-in ready and furnished. Lynn had made up the beds with clean sheets and blankets. She even stocked the cupboards with food. One room had all our boxes neatly stacked in a corner, floor to ceiling. We were home.

Our friends continued to ask us when we were coming back to where we belonged. A few couldn't resist telling us we were crazy. Yet, everything had fallen into place, signs that God had given us the green light. He was behind this move. Still, we had no job, no savings, and no transportation. But, despite a few caveats, there was peace. Every day, our life was like a vacation while we adapted to new sights, sounds, and breathtaking views.

What God starts; He finishes. I knew God would never leave or forsake us. In His timing, everything would continue to fall into place. I was certain.

A few days after we arrived, Mark got a job working for the same company he had worked for in New York. For a short time, he rode the bus to work. Soon we were approved for a brand-new car. A significant shift from the five years of buying one clunker after another. The trajectory of our lives had changed.

I admit. I missed my family and called my mom each week for a long time to enjoy her company. Despite that, the mountains offered indescribable joy. I started each day with a sense of awe bathed in the splendor of God's beauty. His presence permeated this place. God was close and personal. The majestic stature of the elevations humbled me and brought peace to my heart in a way I had not explored. Triggers come and go, and even decades later, I still experience it as if yesterday. Visiting mountains or photographs of mountains can transport me to that place of contentment.

One thing I hadn't prepared for was the religious culture. The Mormons eagerly invited us into their circles.

It surprised me to learn later from many "transplants" that they were shunned as outsiders. It was never the case for us. We loved God and wanted a similar wholesome lifestyle for our children, so we fit right in. They did not snub us, even with the differences in religious doctrine.

I won't say it was trial-free living in a new state. The move would become one of the most significant tests of my life and led to much sorrow. But it was all part of God's perfect plan to guide me back to Him, stronger than ever.

When people ask where I'm from, I was born in NY and raised in Utah. I found myself in the mountains. I walked from darkness into a light where everything about me and life suddenly made sense. I belonged there more than anywhere else I had ever been. Everything felt right.

In retrospect, I see Utah taught me about servanthood. I observed my new Mormon friends lavishing me with love in a new way. Through actions rather than words. Unselfish in giving their time to others, even to their hurt. They worked together to help anyone in need, whether watching my kids so I could take a nap, helping with laundry, making meals, or even putting a roof on someone's home.

I learned to love God with a servant's heart. Raised Catholic, I loved God and learned about Him throughout my childhood. Still, service was on the back burner after all the rosaries, and I checked off the weekly confession. We served, but it felt different.

I never joined the Mormon church, but God used them to draw me into a relationship with Him. I am thankful for the kind souls who walked as disciples, showing me how to love people with actions.

I don't deserve Heaven, and service will not grant me entrance. Only by the grace and the blood of Jesus. As His blood covers us, we eventually want to be like our Father.

I am grateful to the messenger who asked us to move. Beholden to the one who sent that messenger. And thanks to all the people I met in Utah who continued to point me to Jesus.

What a wonderful God we serve! I am thankful that he sees the entire plan and around every corner when we can't.

He Speaks to Redirect Us

Some say that growth and change are painful, but nothing is more painful than being stuck where you don't belong. That can be true of location, job, circles of friends, and even being stuck in a cycle of attitude or perception that doesn't do us any good or honor God.

God is constantly molding us into the image of Christ. Sometimes we can't imagine how we will ever be complete, but He knows what changes we must make to get us where we are going. Often, He sends people into our lives to help us grow into who we truly are.

As a Junior, I recall getting lost in math. My attitude got so bad I became discouraged and emotionally fled the class. I didn't want to take part and stopped turning in homework. My view of myself (and those looking in) was the epic loser. The effect of my actions and attitude left me with a failing grade in that class, and if I didn't pass, I wouldn't graduate, either. I didn't realize the seriousness of my choices. Luckily, God sees who we are even when we can't see ourselves. He sent an excellent teacher onto my path who believed in me and took a chance. A teacher I initially thought I hated but grew to love and respect.

It was a final test week. Since I had no classes, I acted silly, loitering in the halls with my friends and doing everything girls do to waste time. My teacher approached me with a proposal. If I studied with him, he was sure he could help me pass the class. I didn't want to leave my girlfriends, but deep down, I always tried to be dependable and wanted to do the right thing. Minutes later, I found myself in the same classroom that gave me nightmares. *What was I thinking? I agreed to agonize over math problems.* Really? Was this how I wanted to spend my afternoon? No, but for the first time that year, I understood. It was as if a light had turned on. The next day I took the test and, to my surprise, got an 88, which would count multiple times in the grading curve.

Because of my teacher's guidance, one test score lifted my final grade to a 66, just passing. Through the grace of God, I made it.

What would have resulted had that teacher not seen potential in me or crossed my path in the hall that day? No doubt I would have failed that math test. One test would have led me down a different road.

To transform our lives often takes tiny steps rather than significant reversals. These small steps will often lead to big transformations. A simple change in direction, a new way to approach a problem. Faith in yourself. If we open ourselves to accepting and pursuing an alternative path, God will make our necessary changes. Are you ready to try something new?

"Forget the former things; do not dwell on the past. See, I am doing a new thing! Now it springs up; do you not perceive it? I am making a way in the desert and streams in the wasteland."

(NIV) Isaiah 43:18-19

Prayer

Father, thank You for keeping my life in motion. As I am tempted to cling to and dwell in the familiar, grant me wisdom and courage to see You constantly at work on my behalf to move me forward. Allow me to see that all change You command in my life will help me grow and become the person You made me.

In Jesus' name. Amen.

REFLECTION

Think of a time when you did something outside your comfort zone. Write about your experience.

_____

_____

_____

_____

_____

_____

_____

Why do you think God gives us the direction to move forward?

_____

_____

_____

_____

_____

_____

Have you ever been called to do something out of the ordinary?

_____

_____

_____

_____

_____

_____

_____

_____

_____

Think about a time you received unmerited favor and doors opened for you?

_____

_____

_____

_____

_____

_____

_____

_____

_____

JOURNAL YOUR STORY

HE SPOKE

CHAPTER 3

A Fork in the Road

When a situation seems overwhelming and impossible, we want to do something. Anything. Perhaps the most limiting human fault is our need to see the outcome before we act. Paralyzed, we wait for all the answers before we plunge forward. How will this turn out? Until we are sure, we live on the hamster wheel to nowhere but are comfortable landing where we started.

God doesn't want us to live like that. He asks us to trust in His ability to get us where we must go. He gives us the next step.

We can't imagine the route from A to Z, but God's path is faster than what we can accomplish on our own. Steady, one step at a time. God has an extraordinary way of turning our situation upside down and back into perfect alignment just as He spoke the world into existence. When God speaks, it is good. Awe-inspiring, unpredictable, but His message is always right on time.

In my early thirties, I rethought my career. After realizing that I would not become a successful (and famous) painter, I gave up the dream. To my ongoing humiliation, I mistakenly believe if I *like* to do something, I'll use that skill to make a living. During my budding artist phase, I assumed this but only netted five dollars from a painting I sold at a garage sale. My dream was to work in an exciting creative field, but I worked for a major retailer and wore a smock. If only there were paintbrushes in those pockets.

I ran cash registers, stocked shelves, managed multiple departments (big box) and a boutique store, managing it all from open to close for over fifteen years of my career. I accepted this as my life, and mostly, I loved it. I enjoyed the fast pace, the busy spurts marked by dozens of needy customers asking for help, and the lull when we would catch our breath before starting the cycle again. Retail isn't for everyone, but it seemed to suit me. I prized being needed everywhere at once.

I enjoyed building displays and talking to customers. No two days are ever the same. Not the activities, the customers, or even my hours. This flexible schedule enabled me to appreciate a balance of day and night freedom. Spending a day in the mountains, tackling an impromptu day trip mid-week, or enjoying a Wednesday ladies' night out on the town with my friends. I didn't like the low pay or working grueling hours, including nights, holidays, and weekends. But early in my career, I was happy to trade money for experience. For a little money, I learned everything about running a business. But, wondered when I'd see a return on my investment.

I struggled to make ends meet, so I took on a part-time job working in the kitchen of a retirement home. I had no skill in food service, but I enjoyed feeding elderly people.

I never imagined a server's pay would be less than minimum wage, rounding out to about $2.13 per hour and paid every two weeks. Money didn't add up fast, but

I fell in love with the residents and couldn't bring myself to leave the job. I convinced myself that it was a volunteer gig to justify the salary, and the pay was a stipend for gas allowance. A good cause.

Eventually, I had no choice but to quit. This job defeated the purpose of taking extra work. I needed more money.

I was not aware that God was getting ready to change the course of my life. What I never imagined possible; He was about to manifest with a few swift moves of celestial style. Meanwhile, it was time for me to find another part-time job.

What could a retail guru/food service worker with a bit of dining room experience do for some extra cash? Become a server at a chain restaurant. (I thought.) But as I perused the help wanted section for hospitality and restaurant jobs, I discovered a mislabeled ad seeking a retail associate. That was me!

A closer look revealed that the opportunity was a data entry position working for a large grocery retailer at their headquarters. I hadn't a clue about data entry. Still, I oversaw the POS system for several departments and was skilled in ordering and replenishment. Tracking data couldn't be that much different from entering data. At least that's what I thought. The only problem (and it was a big problem) was that I had zero computer skills. I typed letters on an electric typewriter and had never touched a computer.

I mustered the courage to apply and it shocked me when they interviewed me right away, and nearly keeled over two days later, when they called to make an offer. A formal letter followed, which offered me a full-time position making twenty-five cents more per hour than I received as a department manager at the "Big Box." Responsibility was less than management, but I needed money more than a title.

Everything that made it likely for me to land this job had fallen into place, yet it made no sense for me to leave a ladder going up to take on a new ladder starting on the bottom rung. Despite logic, I took the job. It happened so fast I knew God was up to something.

A little anxious about surrendering my life in retail, I held onto my old job, continuing to work nights and weekends. I hesitated to give up on this job and my coworkers. I wanted to keep the door open just in case. *Would I like to drive downtown every day? And what about the challenging city parking?* So many minor inconveniences to endure, and I needed comfort. This new job was way outside my comfort zone.

Like a baby holding onto their favorite blanket, I kept one foot on each side of the fence. I believe sometimes God lets us do that. It's almost like he humors us while watching and shaking his head. But, if it's His will for us to redirect, He will eventually pick us up and put us on the right side with or without the blanket!

Eventually, my boss at the retail store allowed me to return to an earlier position I'd had with them in AR. This allowed me to give up the nights, and I came in on weekends at 6 a.m. balancing register tills, which I did in four hours. Monday through Friday, I worked for my new employer.

About six months later, I finally surrendered and began working only for the corporate office. The minute I let go of the old job, I knew I was in the center of God's will. My lack of peace was not losing the retail side; it was holding on to what God said was finished. A new direction was in order. God showed me He was using my past to shape my future.

Soon, I was more than proficient on the computer, and my former knowledge of POS systems set the stage for me to manage a department again. This time at almost double my former salary and without the demanding schedule. I enjoyed weekends and holidays off and several extra days like President's Day, and training rendezvous. We enjoyed corporate perks, like product samples and free turkeys at Thanksgiving. It didn't take long to get used to exciting surprises, like spending a workday at a ski lodge! It was a fun place to work and had substantial benefits.

Gratitude was an essential factor in moving to this new level. I loved my former job and was thankful for all it had provided for my family and me. God used everything in that role to train me and springboard me into something similar but better. I would never have discovered a job in a corporate grocery headquarters if I had not heard a small voice telling me it was time to look for my "new" job. Was this golden job created for me? I'd like to think I got it because no one else saw it.

In hindsight, my only regret is not letting go the minute God opened the door to my future. But I had little faith. I clung to my security blanket until God had to pry my fingers off the past and push me in the other direction. Thank goodness for those times when He won't take no for an answer!

In a word spoken to the universe, God aligned everything. I advanced from managing 10 retail departments within one store to overseeing POS setup and functionality that affected 1700 grocery stores among many grocery chains in four states across the US.

God can do more abundantly than we can ever dream possible.

He Speaks to Guide Us

Without purpose and direction, no amount of effort, perseverance, or courage matters. We'll keep spinning back and forth on our hamster wheel until we're tired and finally stop. The end of a ride that took us nowhere and awarded us with nothing.

How often have you wanted to change your life, and nothing changed after all the focus you put on it? I love the movie Tuscan Sun, where Katherine explains to Diane Lane's character, Frances, how life unfolds when you cease speculating about things and get on with your life. She recalls how, as a child, she would comb the grass for lady bugs and find none. But when she fell asleep in the grass, she'd wake up covered with lots of lady bugs.

I believe God works that way. It's often when you've finally conceded and started enjoying your life, blooming where you are planted, that God speaks. You find yourself in a new season of life. That thing you worked so hard to achieve is simply dropped into your lap when you least expect it.

It's happened more times than I can count. I wanted out of an apartment, and just when I made it my own and was loving it, it was time to move. Or I may not have ever wanted to leave my job. Still, just when I was comfortable and making things happen, an opportunity came so I could move on to something more extraordinary.

Our destination seems to change once we redirect our focus on God. He directs us when we finally trust Him and rest in Him.

Isaiah 48:17 says, "I am the LORD your God, who teaches you what is best for you, who directs you in the way you should go."

I know if it were not for God's nudge, I would have never made most of the changes in my life. And thankfully, the ones I wanted so badly didn't come to pass.

The prophet Jeremiah reads a letter to the captives in Babylon and tells them, "Build houses and dwell in them; plant gardens and eat their fruit."

There are times we must get serious about the season we're in and simply live. Surrender to where God has led us and look for the blessings. Make the best out of each moment.

God has a plan. Pray for direction. Listen. Follow. But be patient throughout the journey. It could come quickly, or it may take years, but the answer will come. The answer is there before we ask.

"For I know the thoughts that I think toward you, says the Lord, thoughts of peace and not evil. To give you a future and a hope." Jeremiah 29:11

"And I will bring the blind by a way that they knew not; I will lead them in the paths that they have not known: I will make darkness light before them and crooked things straight. These things will I do unto them, and not forsake them.

Isaiah 42:16

Prayer

Father, forgive me when I don't trust in Your wisdom and ability to lead me higher. You are the Alpha and the Omega, the author and finisher of my life. You have carved out a path for me; I need only to walk in it.

In Jesus' name. Amen.

REFLECTION

Think about a time God unexpectedly opened a door. Describe the situation.

_____

_____

_____

_____

_____

_____

_____

Have you ever sensed God wanted you to change directions?

_____

_____

_____

_____

_____

_____

_____

Recall your emotions. How did you respond?

_____

_____

_____

_____

_____

_____

_____

_____

_____

_____

_____

_____

_____

_____

_____

_____

_____

_____

_____

JOURNAL YOUR STORY

_____

_____

_____

_____

_____

_____

_____

_____

_____

_____

_____

_____

_____

_____

_____

_____

_____

_____

_____

_____

_____

HE SPOKE

CHAPTER 4

My Heart's Desire

The Bible says, "Delight yourself in the Lord, and He will give you the desires of your heart." I used to assume that meant whatever I wanted I'd get. Not exactly. I've found He will plant His desires in us, and we want what God wants. Sometimes an enhanced version of what we asked for.

I've always dreamed of becoming a writer. I'd travel around the world with a camera around my neck, capturing the essence of beautiful places and the heroes that lived there. I also wanted to write children's books. Even cookbooks. I've tucked away all those manuscripts in a box, including my first cookbook—filled with cheesecake recipes, which cursed me with high cholesterol. To this day, I've stopped eating eggs overall and eat cheese secretly. Some habits are hard to resist.

In my early writing days, the rejections arrived faster than the manuscripts went out. After a year of hopeful enthusiasm, even "Positive Polly" had to put down the pen and pad and surrender to the painful truth that writing wasn't in the cards for me.

So, I settled. I put my dream on the shelf and joyfully engaged in an uncreative business career. But God continued putting things in order and carved out a seamless chain of events that would allow me to do just that—write.

When the sting of failure wore off, I was at it again. This time writing a novel for teens. I sat up late and rose early to write before and after work, even bringing my project to the office to continue writing during my breaks and at lunchtime. When I finished the first draft, my business career took an abrupt turn I had not expected, which forced my writing to the back burner again.

I learned my employer was moving from a quaint historical one-level structure to a glass highrise downtown. This would be the third office location since I started the job. Excited and scared, I toted all my belongings to the next office building. Soon after settling into the new space, things shifted. Moving "on up" was an understatement. Oiled with favor, my supervisors tapped me for multiple promotions.

But soon the company announced another move. This time operations would be split between two obscure states with acres of potato fields or barren desert... take your pick. *Uh, how about neither?*

Since neither option enticed me, I didn't know what that meant for me, except losing the job I thought would steer me to retirement. Still, I remained loyal to the end. For some odd reason, I had feelings of peace mixed with excitement, an oil and vinegar blend that separated now and then. I believed this change would bring something useful to my life on most days, but I never realized how amazing it would all turn out.

"Why all the glum faces?" My usual Monday face of cheer was even more annoying to them today. And there wasn't any suitable pep talk to respond to the indifferent negative attitudes I'd encountered.

"Oh, you didn't hear? The company is closing this location. Say goodbye to your job next year," my coworker said with sarcasm.

Wow. I was shocked but wanted to learn more. To my surprise, I bounced back from the newsflash with an upbeat reply, "That's exciting! Brand new possibilities."

Like the ears the message fell upon, I couldn't believe I said it. I wondered if my inner child was emerging. That girl who, in former days, lived boldly on the rim of truth. Did I look forward to this change? Surely we would move into a new building and everything would be fine.

"Yeah, the possibility of unemployment," she said.

Still, it was over 12 months away. Anything was possible in a year. 365 days was a long time. I didn't want to get sucked into the pit they had freely jumped into. My coworkers were behaving like this was happening tomorrow. I refused to join them.

Job opportunities waited for me. I would find them. Meanwhile, the rest of the staff put their head in the sand and counted the days. Doom was already on their doorstep. I suspect that's why I was among a handful of managers to lock the doors on the last day. Instead of accepting defeat, I took advantage of every opportunity the company offered to give me a hand up after the split. I signed up for training classes, including resume writing, outplacement, and coaching services. God called the shots, and I trusted this would turn out well for me.

Our last elevator ride was the longest. None of us were ready to say goodbye. Friendships would fall by the wayside. Long-distance communication would dwindle as our lives settled in new directions.

"What are your plans?" I asked Donna, who was the

first person I'd met three years earlier when we moved to the final downtown location. She was from Maine, and I was from New York, and we somehow hit it off in the wild west. She brought me home to reality by hook or by crook, and I tried to enlighten her with positivity. We met somewhere in the middle. Although she told me daily that my positive attitude was unrealistic, I refused to accept too much realism, which was plain cynical.

"Going back to Portland," she said.

I didn't understand why anyone would want to live in the cloudy northeast when the west was a sunny, bubbly place of happiness. But the company had offered all the transferred employees from around the country paid relocation to their hometowns or a city of their choice. So, it finally made sense that anyone who lacked the positivity gene would yearn to get out of the sun.

"You?"

She responded in a tone that I translated as *I don't care*, but I answered anyway.

"Hmm... starting a business."

"A business? What kind of business?"

"A virtual business writing and helping business owners with daily tasks. Like an admin who works from home."

I saw the smirk on her face. Uh, huh... Unspoken questions I heard out loud... *Have you ever started a business? Do you have money to start a business? Will you be able to earn a living with this company?* My mind mouthed the answers to the last two questions. No. But I had worked on my own before, and in my spirit, I believed I would do it again. I didn't know how. Clueless, with no money or experience, I would be a business owner in the next chapter and do what I loved. Writing business letters but writing with the hope, I could break into the freelance writing world on the side. The magazine opportunities awaited. I thought.

My well-meaning elevator chums chuckled and told

me they would catch up with me soon enough at the unemployment lines when I'd be desperate for money and homeless like the rest.

"Don't bet on it," I said.

My journey was difficult, and I had to admit that in the secret recesses of my mind, I heard those evil voices trying to tell me my friends were right... this would not work. I should have picked between desert and potatoes.

After a month in business, all I had to show was a sheet of paper pinned to the wall. The heading read *"Diana's Published Work."* It even had numbered lines all the way down. I had intended to fill blank lines despite a giant pile of reject letters, proving I was a horrible writer, and no formal training or payment, which backed it up. Writers get assignments by showing clips. But how would I get *one*?

Rather than wait for the phone to ring, I overcame the writing gig challenge by offering my services pro bono. I soon discovered that about anyone will give a newbie writer a chance when money wasn't part of the deal. I used one article on the other to gain the next assignment. Each time filling a title into one line on my sheet.

Days rolled into weeks and months, and I worked full time in my home office doing nothing profitable. I had not landed one paid assignment except for developing a sales report for a district sales manager of Big Lots, which paid $86. I couldn't call that spreadsheet assignment writing.

Soon after, I landed my first writing contract (slave labor), creating resumes for an online writing mill that paid me $20 for each one. Finally, the resume classes and outplacement training made sense. But demanding projects required a fast turnaround time, and the money was not worth the sleep deprivation.

I struggled to pay my car payment and took on a job delivering several newspaper routes to pull in extra revenue each month. This required rising at 2 a.m., bundling the papers, and getting out the door at 4 a.m., to perfectly place the papers by 6 a.m. according to each customer's request. Later, I added afternoon routes and a mega volume Sunday paper that practically tore off my left arm after hurling them out the window week after week. But I was determined to keep my weekdays free for the writing gigs. Until one day, a "friend" told me he didn't think this business idea was working.

"It will work. God hasn't revealed everything yet. I believe He said to move forward." My response bordered on the defensive.

"I'm sorry, I don't think you can do it." He laughed under his breath, trying to hold it back, but I didn't miss his intent to humiliate me.

My gut told me to react. I wanted to tell this friend he was stupid. What did he know about starting or running a business? All I said was, "Watch me." The truth hurt me, and a seed of doubt crept in, but I refused to quit.

My trust in God must have hit a switch in heaven because the universal energy shifted. Five months in and I received a surprising call, a man from Greece. I was boggled. Greece? As in halfway around the world, Greece?

I thought it was a joke. How on earth did he get my number? But God has a way of speaking to everyone who He assigns to our plan. The man inquired if I'd write a proposal for his board meeting. Inside, I am laughing out loud. Woah. This was far out of my comfort zone. *Okay, you want me to write a board-level proposal for your business meeting, and who did you say you are?* I was talking to a Vice President of a major global company. What could I say?

"Yes, I can," I told the stranger with the charming accent. We talked about the details, and he emailed me the information, and I headed to the Western Union to pick up the cash payment for this job. A project I did not understand how to start, let alone finish.

Within hours, I broke into panic mode. No, I could NOT do this. Yet, somehow, through God's divine help, I finished it; to my shock, my client loved it.

When God says you are qualified, believe it. He equips the call. That job led to a long-term business relationship with this executive after he asked me if I'd develop his resume. Not just any executive, the division head of a major global company, armed with staff in his own office better equipped to do this than me. Why did he ask me? A woman he had never met, who lived over 6,300 miles away.

My response?

I thought about it. I had written many resumes. I'd done it dozens of times for $20. My "famous painter mentality" kicked in. After all, he offered to pay me $300. Choking on my words, I repeated my usual reply. "Yes, I can. I can write your resume."

Then God put me in the back seat and strapped me in. Had I been positioned anywhere near the steering wheel; I'd have messed this one up. I set out to be an admin, writing and assisting business owners with documentation. God repositioned me toward being a writer helping executives with bios and resumes to support them in promoting themselves. As a specialist writing executive resumes, it positioned me to land a lucrative resume writing contract. It also opened an association with career industry professionals who gave me a break to penetrate new markets and get paid published work. This led to my resumes in over 12 books, features in two career books, and dozens of career-related magazine articles. Eventually, I landed a gig as a journalist for a local newspaper. It gave me the liberty of drumming up all the stories about the heroes I had wanted to write about in the early days.

I still remember the day I looked at the publishing list and realized it had grown to several double-sided pages. It was a miracle, and I know I had nothing to do with it. God charted my steps and guided me along the way.

Fast forward over the last years, and it's been one turn after another, leading me on a voyage to give me the skill I needed for each new assignment. God prepared me for every step of the journey as a writer, and now a publisher.

When God speaks, He doesn't always tell us what he's up to or where we're headed. It's like putting my little hand in his big hand and walking through a thick fog. Then He whispers, we're going left now; turn right now. The security in knowing you heard Him say, keep going, is all we need when naysayers appear.

He will fulfill the desires of your heart, but He always trains us first in His timing. Then He takes what you want to do and makes it more amazing than you can imagine.

He Speaks to Inspire Us

Mark Twain said, "The two most important days of your life are the day you were born and the day you find out why."

Have you thought about your purpose? The clue is in that deep desire toward something. You may have felt called and are already in a successful career or pursuing that direction. Or you may engage as a hobby or pastime. But you constantly find yourself attracted to that one thing. It's where time stands still. You are working effortlessly with delight. Often, it's said to be that thing you would do for free.

For me, it's always been writing and artistic pursuits. I loved drawing and painting and exploring art as a photographer, but mostly I loved creating and designing.

Decades before the age of computers, I discovered a passion for making newsletters for my girl scout troop. I would create the articles on my electric typewriter and cut them out and place them strategically on the page. Far into the wee hours of the night, I'd be cutting apart the stories and clip art and carefully placing the articles and art on the page. I'd cover them with transparent tape to ensure the lines would not show when I printed the finals. I loved how I could create the design and make it everything I wanted it to be. This led to my love of scrapbooking.

40 years later, I would not immediately connect the two. I was asked to take over the newsletter production for my employer. And this time, with computers and colorful graphics to make the entire process easier and even more exciting. The earlier years were a preparation for what I'm doing today. I still love doing it. The entire project scope, creating a theme, working up a cover, and formatting all the information and ideas to bring it all together, then publishing that month's issue for everyone to see.

This is perhaps why I now take it a step further and write books, and help others publish their books. I get a vision for a book cover and recruit someone to help me bring that to life. I think of ideas for a book concept and write my thoughts in a notebook. The thoughts come fast and often land on post-it notes, but they ultimately make it into a book. We do what we are made to do.

Leon Brown says that we betray our true selves if we do not follow our heart's desire. "For what the heart is attracted to is your destiny," he says.

Have you found your destiny?

"A man's heart devises his way: but the Lord directs his steps."

Proverbs 16:9

Prayer

Father, I am so glad You see me differently than I perceive myself. You made me and put desires and interests in my heart. I am grateful as I plan my way; you are faithful to let me see the vision You have prepared for me, which will always amaze me compared to the pale version I carve out for myself. Speak. I want to hear You.

In Jesus' name. Amen.

REFLECTION

Think about some desires you've had in your early years. How many have you achieved? Or have your desires changed?

_____

_____

_____

_____

_____

_____

_____

Write about a time God was preparing you for the future. You may not have realized it, but later it may have become apparent.

_____

_____

_____

_____

_____

_____

_____

Has a situation ever tempted you to quit but you kept going
and ultimately found success?

_____

_____

_____

_____

_____

_____

_____

_____

_____

_____

_____

_____

_____

_____

_____

_____

_____

_____

_____

JOURNAL YOUR STORY

HE SPOKE

CHAPTER 5

The Eleventh Hour

Now and then, you know the word you've received is WAIT. No matter what language we hear, it means the same, do nothing.

In this crazy world of instant gratification and trying to manipulate the outcome of every situation, it can be a tough pill to swallow. I had plenty of friends urging me to move.

"When do you need to be out?"

"Two weeks," I said.

"Two weeks! You haven't found a new place. You're not packed. Where will you go?"

I had to admit; I was cutting it close. A single mom with two kids at home, I had obligations. Recalling that time, I wonder if their tender hearts were worried. They never expressed it. Or maybe I wasn't paying attention. Perhaps they tried to take care of me. I'm sure they saw right through my charade. I hid a lot of things, trying to keep everything looking sane. But, how rational does it look when you're out of heating oil and trying to explain to your kids we're sleeping in our coats tonight?

The icy cold spell in Virginia had begun. We struggled that winter. Sometimes it was bitter cold, and all the heating oil I could afford was a $20 gas can of diesel fuel I picked up at Sheets to keep the furnace running through the night.

The fuel company required a $200 minimum order, so we got by paycheck to paycheck buying fuel in the small increments, using it only at night.

Through the grace of God, we survived, and spring was fast approaching. I had given my official notice, and we had to be out of the rental by March 15. There were many reasons we wanted to move. The house was affordable but falling apart. And it wasn't in my daughter's elementary school district. But mostly, we needed a place to build fresh memories. I had just two weeks to find a new home for my kids and then figure out how to pack our entire life into an old Chevy, unload it, and settle into a new life. From anyone's perspective, IMPOSSIBLE.

My income was limited to a starving writer's salary. With no child support or savings, I couldn't pay for a moving company. My sister had even offered to "save" me by sending her husband to pick us up in a U-Haul and bring us to California to get us on our feet and we could move wherever we wanted afterward. Tempting, but I felt called to stay.

Although what I had decided seemed foolish to everyone, including myself, I felt at peace. On the outside, I was nervous. Things were crazy, but I believed God had asked me to wait. An answer was coming.

I kept searching and praying, but nothing turned up. Days passed, and time was running out. In retrospect, I'm glad the searches had failed because I may not have had the courage to wait if God had not closed all the surrounding doors. I felt as if I was walking down a dark hallway with locked doors and a faint light at the end. I sensed God working behind the scenes, and I hoped I would be patient. When would a door open? Would I have the courage to wait?

After Church on Sundays, we would drive through the neighborhoods to look for rent signs. Each week we came up empty. Houses we loved were too expensive or required too much deposit up front. And we had a dog.

Not very hopeful, we took another drive to an area we had scoured the week prior. I saw a couple of new signs. Called one and got a recording. The second sign said *House for Rent* with a phone number. I called it, and the man said he could show it right away. It was a short drive to the school my daughter wanted to attend.

We drove up to an adorable older brick home built in the forties. It had three bedrooms and was the perfect size for our family. A beautiful, fenced backyard big enough for a small pool. A storage shed, and an attic increased the square footage. My heart soared as we roamed through the house. It was more than a house. Even empty, it was a real home, and it was already ours.

That meeting ended with the property owner letting me sign the contract on the spot and he even allowed a few extra days to clear out of the old house and settle into the new one. The rent was reasonable, and he worked with us on the security deposit to keep our dog.

That night we celebrated like lottery winners. Still, there were hurdles to cross before we could realize our dream of a fresh start in a new home. Getting our furniture into this house would be a major challenge.

So, when my friends continued to ask why I hadn't packed, what else could I say? It wasn't a moving day. But also, I tend to be a procrastinator. I also believe God's timing is not our timing, and I wasn't sure how He had planned to work this out. But I didn't want to live in a stack of boxes until I discovered it.

"You realize on March 15 you are closing these doors for the last time?"

"I know."

It was true. I suffer from planning paralysis. Don't move until the plan unfolds. Did that mean I didn't trust God? I couldn't see His method, so I sat still, waiting and waiting, falling back on my warped sense of *trust*. In retrospect, I wonder if genuine faith would have been packing while not seeing anything unfold before me. Would that have sped up the process?

March 10 rolled around, and I had no inkling how I would move our stuff. I was close to pushing panic mode with fingers crossed behind my back, but I kept a cheerful face for my kids. Amid my poker face, I pretended to pack, but still didn't know how this would all turn out. So, on Friday afternoon when I picked up my daughter from school, I took a chance.

"Valerie, do you know any men at the church who might have a pickup truck to help me move furniture?"

Although Saturday was short notice, she told me about her friend who had started a weekend moving ministry to support the elderly and widows who needed help. A single mom would fall in line with their criteria.

"His name is Tom. I'll call him and see if he can help," she said.

Tom would email his crew, but he didn't know if anyone would get the message so late on a Friday. But, when God has a plan worked out for you in advance, you can bet He's already told His crew where to be and what to do regarding His plan. Not only did all the guys see the email, but no sooner than Tom hit send, he began receiving replies. He called to give me the good news.

"Diana?"

"Yes."

"This is Tom from the church. We'll have a crew at your house at 8:30 a.m. tomorrow." That was four days before the cutoff.

With nothing left to do but cry, I hunched over and hugged myself as I felt the steady release of tension like letting air out of a balloon. I sat, drenched in tears, crying until I could cry no more. I was humbled and grateful. My God had come through. He who promised to provide was faithful.

The following day, the trucks arrived. Through misty eyes, I watched in amazement as an orchestrated fleet of vehicles pulled up in a symphony, one right after the other. Within two hours, everything from the old house was on a truck, and they drove us to our new home etched with a brand-new future.

After putting every piece of furniture in its place, we formed a circle, and the kind men prayed with us and over us. They prayed through all the rooms of the house and blessed our well-being in that home. What they did for us was one of the most sacrificial acts of love I'd ever seen. So generous. So much love. Words cannot describe the emotions that went through me that day.

Strangers loved my kids and me. They were the hands and feet of Jesus' carrying and caring for us and all our things. They placed everything right where it belonged and didn't leave until we were all tucked in safely.

They wouldn't take money or even eat refreshments I had for them. They had a job to do.

This is one time I'm so glad I listened as He spoke. *"Be patient, my child. I've got this."*

He Speaks to Answer Us

After years of praying, I've realized that sometimes the best answers come during times (we think) He's not listening. God is not a genie who pops up after we say a few magic words, do a little dance, or rub a little pot.

God is looking for faithful followers who seek Him in good times and bad. But more important, will trust in Him. In everything. He will provide all that we need in due time. Sometimes the delays we are facing are merely the preparation we need to do that next thing, meet that person, or go where He is leading. Sometimes it's because we aren't doing what he's asking. Either way, the road may be rocky but remember that His ways are not ours and His timing is no on our schedule.

Hebrews 11:6 says, "But without faith, it is impossible to please Him, for he who comes to God must believe that He is and that He is a rewarder of those who diligently seek Him."

And sometimes, that comes packaged in the word, NO.

"Commit thy way to the Lord; also trust in Him, and He shall bring it to pass."

- Psalm 37:5

Prayer

Father, I know you care about me and understand what I need. Thank You for all the times You didn't give me what I thought I needed. But, mostly, thank You for the times I patiently waited for You to bring what I needed to pass. Forgive me when I am anxious. You know the plans for me. When I am tempted to run ahead of You, kindly pull me back. My trust is in You.

In Jesus' name. Amen.

REFLECTION

Think about a time you experienced a problem too big for you to handle? What did you do?

_____

_____

_____

_____

_____

_____

_____

When is it most difficult for you to trust God?

_____

_____

_____

_____

_____

_____

_____

In what ways have you let go of control and allowed God to intervene in your problems?

_____

_____

_____

_____

_____

_____

_____

_____

_____

_____

_____

_____

_____

_____

_____

_____

_____

_____

_____

_____

_____

JOURNAL YOUR STORY

HE SPOKE

_____

_____

_____

_____

_____

_____

_____

_____

_____

_____

_____

_____

_____

_____

_____

_____

_____

_____

_____

_____

_____

_____

CHAPTER 6

Chasing Squirrels

I f you asked me twenty years ago where I could find happiness, I'd tell you, the mall. My theory was wrong. I believed that my happiness meter would rise within concrete buildings filled with shiny trinkets.

Material things are meaningless without people to share them with. Scattered along the journey, are the real gifts. Treasures of moments and memories that stir our hearts and forever change us. People come into our lives, sometimes for a brief appearance and others for a season, and some remain with us for a lifetime. George stayed for more than a season and will remain in my heart forever.

My youngest daughter was the first to meet him. It was our move-in day, and I struggled with an armload of boxes as I saw her standing by the fence talking to an elderly man. Stranger danger speech rolled right off her.

"Come and meet George!" she called, proud of her encounter. Kate collected people like marbles. She had a way of making friends with every stranger she met. She'd make friends at the grocery checkout, post office, anywhere people mingled. She liked people and considered everyone she met her friend. I found that same quality in George.

He extended his friendship and invited us to his house to chat. It delighted me to take a break but also to get to know my new neighbor. George welcomed us with a hearty, "Come on in!" Even on a weekday, the elderly gentleman dressed for church, wearing a white button-up collared shirt and dress pants belted high above his waist. He stood tall, holding a cane in one hand while reaching out with the other to shake my hand. I wasn't prepared for a handshake that gripped me so tightly it nearly knocked me off my feet. He was a youngster, no doubt masquerading as an 85-year-old. He'd be helping me lug groceries from the car. I was sure.

I felt an instant connection with George and his wife. A native Virginian with southern charm, George was the leader of his house. He loved his family and still cherished his wife as he did from the moment he laid eyes on her. George's eyes lit up each time he spoke of her. Irma was a sprite woman several years younger than her husband. Always well dressed and busy trekking around town, doing many things for her children and her church.

George treated us like family. I don't remember our friendship growing. It just always was. We frequently spent time at their home relaxing in the afternoons and evenings. We enjoyed simple chats, talking about everything from his childhood experiences, navy life, and the day he decided he would never eat tongue again. George always had a story to tell, and many involved the Great Depression or eating oysters on a navy ship. He always made us laugh.

He loved showing off his backyard patio. He often invited us to watch the squirrels run around the yard and up a 50-year-old tree that George reminded everyone *he* planted. It was his tree. Irma wanted it removed because the leaves were a challenge to rake, but he would not allow that to happen, not during his lifetime. I'd often peek out the kitchen window and see him sitting back there on his lawn chair watching the stars and the moon, even in a thunderstorm, especially in a storm. George loved to watch the rain and listen to the thunder.

For nine years, I enjoyed our special friendship and found him a man of character who loved God and expressed gratitude daily. He appreciated everything and everyone. George often told me all he ever wanted was a family. The Lord had given him a beautiful wife, a home, and a job to care for his family, and he couldn't have asked for more. He had gotten everything he wanted in life and took great care to cherish it.

George valued people. He cared for his siblings, and as the oldest, God granted him the longest life, surpassing them all. I suppose because he understood and cared for them and was Godly appointed to watch over them. They needed him, as we did.

On a sad day, a car killed our dog, George comforted us, but he and his wife also handled the grizzly details, which we were in no shape to manage ourselves. They didn't ask us; they stepped in. Something real friends do. Genuine love never asks if someone needs help. It shows up.

"I don't know how to tell her, George," I said, crying.

My son was sobbing nonstop on the side of the road where our beautiful white dog lay in a pool of blood. Moments before, he saw the gate wide open and ran to find Rocco, but too late.

This dog, my daughter, had picked for herself when we lived 2,000 miles across the country, and we had brought him to Virginia four years before. A little pink spot on his nose was the only distinguishing factor that made her choose him out of a liter of white bundles of fur. What made this puppy even more special to Kate was that he was the offspring of her first dog, Kiska. She had suffered the same fate as Rocco. That awful day, Kate watched her dog's death as it ran in front of a truck while she was running to greet her father.

Soon after Kiska died, Rocco escaped his own death as a pup after he fell on a hard surface. The veterinarian advised us to put the puppy down; he would not make it. Kate's father had refused to do it and asked for painkillers, and he nursed the dog back to life. He was determined to do all he could for the dog with the cute spot on his nose.

After several weeks of care, his efforts paid off, and Rocco was a lively and energetic puppy once again. Kate loved him more than ever. At five years old, she would dress him in a matching t-shirt and call him "her brother." Now I struggled with how to tell her the second dog she loved was dead.

George remained with us when Kate got off the school bus that day. We all held her tight as he told her the truth. It was a heartbreaking moment for all of us. For weeks we all mourned for Rocco. Even me, who had only now come to appreciate the warmth he provided my legs as he lay beside me every morning while I worked at my computer.

Life offers celebrations and sorrows. All are best enjoyed with friendships of the heart. George was in my heart. We enjoyed him in good times and bad. But I wasn't prepared for the worst.

"I have bad news to tell you," Kate said as we sat at the Egg & I for breakfast one morning. This young woman, who had given herself the childhood nickname of "I love," didn't seem very heartbroken. Still, my interest was piqued, but I didn't jump into worry mode. I expected unfortunate news, like she had decided a job change was in order. She was looking for a new apartment, or she had wrecked her car.

"What is it?" I leaned forward.

"George died. The day after Thanksgiving. I saw it on Facebook." She reminded me of how often I had wanted to visit George but didn't. How often I had worried about his health, tormented by the possibility that something had happened to him. And today, I learned all those times–2 ½ years, he was alive, and I did not visit him. I prayed and asked God to let me see him again. God answered, leaving that door wide open while He waited for me to walk through it. Then He closed it. An opportunity lost. Days stretched into weeks, into months and years, until it was too late.

One day Kate shared with me she had driven with friends to look at our old house and saw lots of cars at George's home. They posted a sign on the property about oxygen in use. I feared the worst. George stopped responding to my cards. I worried he had passed. Yet, I couldn't bring myself to check into it. Thinking back, I realize our phone numbers may have changed, so I'm not sure if he could answer. Usually, we'd receive a return call or a card. Eventually, it would lure us to take the trip and visit our beloved friend.

I never stopped loving George. He was the same age as my maternal grandfather, who had passed when I was 13. It didn't take long for me to realize, The Lord had blessed me with this man to assume a grandfather role in my life.

When I remarried and moved away from the neighborhood, he and his wife attended our wedding. George visited us at our new home several times with his wife and even after she passed. We continued to see him, particularly on birthdays and Christmas, which was twice every December.

But our visits became more sporadic when Kate had taken a job in a fast-food chain, and I had accepted a new role managing events. The new job entirely swept the rug out from under me, as I had never realized it would consume so much of my time. The hours were not only long, but they kept me working until late in the evening, which eliminated weekday visits with my friend. With only one day off per week, we soon made fewer trips. After Kate graduated from high school, I found it even more challenging to take the 30-minute drive. When she moved into her own apartment, we stopped going altogether.

Kate's and my schedule conflicted, and my excuse was always we never had the time to go *together*. She continued to tell me to go by myself. I regret I didn't go alone. I regret I didn't verify he was alive and well. I regret I did not give the most valuable gift I offered, the gift of friendship, to my friend in his time of need.

I had taken my friend for granted and not expressed to him my sincere care for him. I couldn't have loved him any less than my blood relatives, yet he didn't know. I worried that something had happened to him. I worried more about myself; if I could handle the deep sorrow. I worried about how I would feel if they would reveal his demise after knocking on his door for a random visit. I should have called. But I chose not to trust God. Trusting God means leaving the consequences to Him, knowing He will get us through anything.

George's obituary mentioned a dear friend that had been with him in his time of greatest need. Reading those words pierced my heart knowing it was not me. We went from regularly caring about our friend and checking in on him to no contact. I wonder what he thought about us vanishing from his life. Did he ever ask about us? Did he read the cards I sent? He was cognizant because his last day on earth was spent enjoying Thanksgiving with his family. Bop Bop's last day was spent in precisely the way he would have wanted. Loving his family, enjoying a delicious meal, and a massive piece of pecan pie. Then they drove him home, and he went to sleep and woke up in eternity.

I miss George. Watching the light in his garage as he peddled five miles on his bike every morning at 5 a.m. Sitting with him on the patio, observing squirrels, or a rainstorm. Talking with him over the fence while our dog, Bella, ran along the wall with his daughter's dog, Dot. Standing on his front porch, waiting for him to answer, and embracing him after a long time apart. And just when I was sure that George would be my forever friend, I broke the friendship chain.

I miss the way he always said goodbye with a warm smile and an eager invitation for us to *come back!* He would always call Kate "Sarg," referring to her connection with the JROTC. George was a Navy man, and they shared a military bond.

Appreciating people is a lesson I often learn the hard way. I've loved many people. Deeply. Yet, I may not have ever expressed how much people mean, and often, the chance is taken from me. Sometimes I wanted to cry and say, *wait, I have something to tell them!* But they're gone. I'm still taking that test because The Lord has repeatedly spoken to my heart and expressed that the people, He has given me were gifts to enjoy, but the ownership belongs to Him. There are no guarantees on how long I'll be able to enjoy them. Only that I must. Today.

I realize I am not aware of how much people mean until they depart. I often want to see people because I have something to say, but the chance doesn't present itself. The truth is, I don't make the time. Sometimes a letter or a phone call is necessary. Instead, I wait for tomorrow when I might take a trip and tell them in person. The magnitude of the loss I feel regarding people and the invaluable price attached to these heavenly gifts is a mystery I am always left to sort out. I'm still taking that test and failing miserably.

Days are precious. Time is a gift. We never know what will happen. Times change, people change, and circumstances have a way of twisting and turning on the road we are on toward a different direction altogether. Unexpected change is the only thing sure. Often, I let the busyness of life hinder appreciating and making time for people I care most about. I'm learning too late that nothing is more important than people.

I've also realized that the blessings we get are fleeting, given to us to enjoy for a season or a chapter. The biggest gifts are not things we can pack in a box and send across the country. The blessings might just be the memories and people you leave behind. The moments of laughter. The times when people encourage us or stand by us when working on something that matters to us.

Maybe some of the greatest blessings are in the neighbor that lives right next door. Have you said hello to them lately?

He Speaks to Bless Us

'Never lose an opportunity of seeing anything beautiful, for beauty is God's handwriting." Ralph Waldo Emerson

I love that quote. God's handwriting. He formed the world with his finger. The world is in His handwriting, yet we fail to read the story. We see the beauty of nature and babies and everything lovely. But when something happens, that isn't so good, we say that it couldn't be God. We rebuke it and try to find our way around it. But learn from it? No.

The scripture promises that nothing happens in our life without God's approval. Meaning His stamp is on it. And when we think about God as the giver of "good gifts," we debate whether or not we believe that. Would a "good" God let me lose this job, house, or friend? Would He want me to get sick? Sometimes. God gives good gifts, and yes, all things are good.

Sometimes blessings come in strange packages. Often, we don't notice the gift because it comes in Cognito, is covered in odd packaging, and is left at the most inopportune times.

For me, it was wrapped in a swollen knee I couldn't walk on for nearly a year and a half. I traipsed from surgeon to surgeon, wanting relief but getting answers I didn't want to hear. A possible surgery. It would be simple. I'd be back on my feet in eight weeks, they said. Eight weeks is a long time when you work in event management during wedding season. More than that, I didn't want to be cut. I'd had enough surgeries with three c-sections and refused to do it again. I suspected this swelling was because of my rheumatoid arthritis, and all I wanted was to drain the knee. I was diagnosed 18 years before and this was the first major flair-up I'd had since the initial onset. But these doctors were not eager to get the fluid out. Instead, they scheduled appointments that gave me little or no relief, and I was left with a swollen knee while they waited on the sidelines putting on the surgeon's gear.

People shook their heads as they watched me limping and dragging my 10-pound leg. They would ask me when I was going under the knife. "You really need to bite the bullet and get that knee fixed," they would say.

Eventually, the other knee swelled, and I had little or no mobility. I walked like an 80-year-old. It was so painful to move from one place to the next that I sat most of the time. I lost muscle tone. I even lost weight because it was a struggle to stand at the counter to even make a sandwich.

But I kept up a good front and came to work each day with a smile on my face. I'd act like it was all okay, and I'd get through it. But at night, alone on my bed, my real feelings would emerge as I cried out to God, sobbing myself to sleep. He would comfort me at this pity party until the wee hours of the night. It's incredible that God even showed up after the first few. But He is faithful. Each time He comforted. We had a great bedtime ritual. I'd sob for an hour, He would hold me in His arms and lull me to sleep, and the next night we'd do it all over again.

Blessing? I was wondering. I was tired, and I wanted to walk again. But I refused to get a walker even though I needed one. I'd place chairs all over the living room so I could cling from one to the other to get to the next room. If that's not living in denial, I don't know what is.

One day limping slowly from my car to my office, something changed. I felt as if God was asking me to look around. I saw everything so vividly. Stunning Crepe Myrtles, birds flying everywhere. The grass was so green. Everything was just beautiful. The smells, the sights, and the sounds. I knew I was blessed to work at a country club surrounded by a beautiful golf course. I wondered why I hadn't seen the magnitude before. I'd always thought it was lovely, but this day, I saw it in a new way. Suddenly I was grateful for what was there despite what I lacked. As I trudged up the hill, I thanked God for allowing me to limp up that hill. He could have given me a wheelchair or worse, but I knew I was blessed to limp.

And suddenly, it hit me that the blessing in this "downtime" was for me to see instead of look. To see blessings amid difficulty. To remember that I can do all things through Christ, and nothing is impossible with God. To be thankful that despite it all, He was with me.

I saw the beauty of being still. Until then, my life rolled by like a blur. I was working crazy long hours with each day running into the next. I couldn't remember what I had for lunch that afternoon. My week was just one long 168-hour day!

All things come from God. We don't know what we will get and how long it will be, a happy time or a difficult chapter. Either way, we must embrace and appreciate all the gifts. We never know how long we will have them. Even inside difficulty, there are a few pleasures to enjoy.

"The Lord giveth, and the Lord taketh away." Job 1:21

Prayer

Father, all good things come from you. And it is all good. The people you have placed in my life are gifts to be borrowed for an indefinite length of time. The challenges you bring are, too, with hidden encouragement and blessing. Help me embrace and appreciate each person and event you have blessed me with, understanding you are in control. Give me the grace to accept and enjoy all things.

In Jesus' name. Amen.

REFLECTION

Recall when someone was taken from you before you were ready to let go?

_____

_____

_____

_____

_____

What would you say to them now if you had one more chance?

_____

_____

_____

_____

What are you thankful for today?

_____

_____

_____

_____

Make a list of ten gifts God has given you? Try to think past the obvious things such as food, shelter, and clothing.

_____

_____

_____

_____

_____

_____

_____

_____

_____

_____

_____

_____

_____

_____

_____

_____

_____

_____

_____

JOURNAL YOUR STORY

CHAPTER 7

Teetering a Fine Line

There have always been days when I talked about trusting God. I told people I believed He would take care of me. I shared many examples of living "bare bones" and waiting patiently for God to usher in His saving grace. I was grateful. But did I believe that, or did a part of me pridefully take credit for my stuff? I was living as a freelance writer, making my schedule, choosing projects. I had something to do with my success, right?

We never know what we believe until we fall into the vat of boiling water, and there's nothing you can do to pull ourselves out. So, we pray. But we hear no answers. And the chaos in our brain becomes so loud that we wouldn't be able to understand anyway if they put the answer to our ear with a megaphone. We keep going in circles, wondering what *we* will do.

I pulled into the parking lot and saw his truck parked across from me. He stared into my eyes. Even at that distance, my eyes burned from the glare. I looked away, pretending not to see him.

Grocery shopping didn't seem like such a good idea. Heart racing, I watched out of the corner of my eye as he waited and observed me as a hunter studies a field for a buck. How long could I sit in the car pretending to keep busy and doing nothing? I lost all courage to get out. This was a tricky situation. I wanted to start the engine and drive away. He would follow me. He had a way of driving sight unseen, even in his monster truck, and then appearing out of nowhere.

If I drove home, he'd meet me there. Going anywhere else would only be a waste of gas and money I could not spare. So, I got out of my vehicle. In harmony, our doors opened and shut. I was about to face my fear.

"I want my money." He was firm, and his tone was angry. This property owner that had once been a Godsend had become my worst nightmare. I didn't blame him. I was two months behind, and there was no chance of employment on the horizon. I had been working freelance writing resumes for a couple years when my computer crashed and left me with projects undone and unstable availability as I tried to work from the library while my daughter was at school. It seemed the more I struggled to stay afloat, the harder it was to keep up my project schedule, and my revenue was shrinking. The company I worked for was losing patience with me and offered fewer projects. I couldn't keep up the pace working limited hours.

"I'm sorry. I promise I'll get it. Just give me a few more days." It was the usual empty promise that never seemed to pan out.

My family had helped as much as they were able. We had sold items from our storage unit. My Sunday school class had collected $300 one month, which was the exact amount I had been short. Another loaned me $600 to keep my electricity until my writing check arrived, which I handed over to him the following week. Repeatedly, a step ahead, two steps back, and sometimes three. I knew this was going nowhere, and I needed a solution, not another band-aid and mini extension. My entire net worth comprised my car, a small dish of coins I was saving for gas, and the stack of Hardee coupons that would be dinner for the next two weeks. I swallowed my pride and called my deacon.

"I'm in trouble. I'm going to be homeless if I don't pay my rent, and I don't know what to do."

We were on the verge of living in my car, and I didn't want to accept this. I kept smiling so my girl wouldn't be worried. And if I held a smile on my face, she'd think everything was just fine. The only actual expenses were food, rent, electricity, and gas, which I had let go to save money. We showered at the fitness center to avoid cold showers. I don't think my daughter cared. She loved going to the gym to swim in the pool, and the bathrooms and showers were fancy, like being on vacation. But losing the gas also meant I couldn't use the dryer or the stove. I hung clothes on hangers and cooked dinner on a hot plate, explaining that the dryer and stove were broken. It was a stretch, but without a connection, they didn't work, which to a kid meant broken. Between the Hardy's coupons and primitive cooking apparatus, we could eat. There were minor adjustments I could make to allow us to live normally. Living in a car was a change I wasn't ready to step into. I held my breath, waiting for a response.

With no hesitation, my deacon told me to consider it done. The church would cut the check, and my landlord could pick it up. I hung up the phone and cried. They had lifted a weight from my shoulders.

Within the next month, I received an offer for a job that quickly grew into full-time. God could have presented a new job right away. But I would have taken credit for that. I wouldn't have realized my need for God, nor understood that He holds it all. He gives us blessings, and He can quickly take them away.

I knew there would be challenges ahead, but the light at the end of the tunnel was brighter. My landlord accepted my new job in good faith and worked with me to get back on track.

Sometimes God lets us wait for Him to see if we'll trust in Him. But God wants us to know we could not have done this thing without Him. We are brought to the place we are humbled enough to accept His help. He provides when we stop trying to help ourselves.

He Speaks to Help Us

We don't always know what we need, but God does. Sometimes we must grow through unpleasant situations. As dark as our situation becomes, in Him, there is no darkness. John Piper said that night comes, and in it, the future looks blank. That's when fear steps in. I think of blank, and I think of nothing. An empty cup, a blank sheet of paper, and an expanse of barrenness. Desolation. The opposite of which is hope, which can only be in God.

We are all faced with situations that present no hope or solution. At least in our power. In that place, we have lost courage and have nothing to pull from. We draw a blank as we struggle to make sense, but we can see no way out.

"Is my arm too short it cannot save?" With God, nothing is impossible. Even when you think you've lost it all.

The car stalled. When I saw black smoke slithering from underneath the hood of my car, I knew it was over. This car would go no farther, but neither would I if I couldn't get a new vehicle fast. I had no money for a down payment and limited credit.

A friend was kind enough to drive us to Car Max, where I found a sporty two-seater, unpractical but a bargain price I could afford. My daughter was swept in by a big SUV with the TV. I instantly saw it loaded with passengers all under four feet tall, blowing bubbles and singing rounds of *The Wheels of the Bus Go Round and Round*. I could see the excitement in her eyes, but there was no way we could afford a full-size SUV. Not even the gas.

We settled on a smaller Ford Escape with leather seats I loved. And it could transport her entourage. Still, I didn't think I'd be able to afford it. For me, it was too fancy. The salesperson assured me I could afford it, so I agreed to let him process the loan. Within a short time, he said we would drive home in a new vehicle.

Three hours later, I had my doubts. I vacillated between disappointment and hope as I prayed. But the loan was declined twice. What usually was a quick process had become a circus event with major hoops to jump through, and it was getting late. My friend was losing patience, but he didn't want to leave me until he knew I was safely approved. The last attempt was to get my writing income verified. It was impossible to do at that late hour, and I needed a car.

So, I continued to pray. Fervently believing that God would not let me down. I reminded the Lord that if He provided no new car, He would have to provide a ride to work. After that, I told the salesperson to rerun the loan with only my full-time income and remove everything hindering us. He agreed but said it would decline because it would be even less income. I felt peace and had resigned myself to whatever happened; it was God's choice. I don't know if more faith or exhaustion led me there.

Within a few minutes, the salesperson came back shaking his head and told us he didn't know how, but we were approved. We were in the blank zone, and God put the story on paper. At midnight, we drove home with a new vehicle, and it was a miracle.

"But my God shall supply all your needs according to His riches in glory by Christ Jesus." Philippians 4:19

Prayer

Father, thank you for loving me and caring for all my needs. Our efforts are in vain when we try to help ourselves. Somehow, during our struggle, we don't see. When we ask for your guidance and trust all the outcomes to You, we come out safely. Happy is the man who trusts in You.

In Jesus' name. Amen.

REFLECTION

Recall a time you faced a problem so big you knew you couldn't face it yourself? What did you do?

_____

_____

_____

_____

In what ways do you try to be self-sufficient?

_____

_____

_____

_____

Think about a time you tried to solve your own problem, and the results were not good? Are there steps God was calling you to take that you avoided?

_____

_____

_____

_____

_____

Recall a time God stepped in when you had lost nearly all hope. What happened?

_____

_____

_____

_____

_____

_____

_____

_____

_____

_____

_____

_____

_____

_____

_____

_____

_____

_____

_____

JOURNAL YOUR STORY

HE SPOKE

CHAPTER 8

It's Not a Hole in God's Eye

"You didn't wear that shirt to work, did you?"

"No. Why would I wear *this* shirt? To work? You know I wear suits to work. Every. Day." It agitated me, and I wasn't in the mood to answer. He'd already asked me this question too often. I knew what would follow.

"Oh. Well, the shirt has a hole in it," my husband replied, as if this news was hot off the press. He is forever pointing out my flaws. The way I do things, the spec of something on my nose, the list goes on. He claims it to be *his job* to "help" me when he's in this mode. Just trying to help. Yet, I sense a slight tinge of sarcasm. He wasn't *ever* going to miss a chance to start a *holey shirt* conversation.

I'm finally where I know I need no man's help to dress. Days like this, I was sure.

Feeling the breeze through the quarter-size puncture just off the shoulder, I knew the shirt had a hole in it. The "clothing patrol" had mentioned this before.

The most comfortable shirt in my closet begged to be worn after a hard day of work. A softly knit navy pullover with a slightly scooped neckline and a wedge of silky patterned fabric sewn at the bottom made it longer and super cozy, with skinny jeans and boots. I loved this shirt. I found it on a clearance rack just a few months before, yet somehow it already had a hole in it. Even at a bargain price, it was too comfortable to give up.

Okay, I'll give you a wee bit of disclosure... My clothes get tears in them a lot. I'm not sure how, but they do. Sometimes within the same week of purchase. And, I have a terrible habit of wearing these clothes despite the holes. Mainly around the house in the comfort of home. We live in the backwoods; who will see me, right?

Okay, full disclosure. I routinely wear clothes (and shoes) with holes in them, even out in public. Before you panic, I'm not talking about visibly torn fabric. Subtle flaws I can usually cover up creatively.

It's not that I can't afford to replace them. Or I don't care about my appearance. I have a history of holding onto comfort. Faded cozy sweaters. Soft sweats with a detached waistband. Blouses without buttons. So familiar, I can't let them go. It would be painful.

Minor flaws. Why replace clothing that fits so comfortably? I'll enjoy them until I can find replacements. If I could find the item (same brand, size, and color), it might incline me to kiss them goodbye. Then I learned the manufacturers stopped making them ten years ago. Yes, I have worn some of my clothes for decades.

So, until I discover another sweater or a pair of sweats, shoes, slippers, as comfortable as the "holey" item, don't mess with my imperfect clothing. I'm keeping them on purpose.

For years, I wore a sweater to cover a ripped sleeve in a favorite blouse. I cherished this blouse and paid a tailor the price of a new shirt to repair it. Replace the blouse? Never. They discontinued it years ago. I'm convinced I need a personal seamstress.

My husband doesn't have this problem. His slightly worn jeans beckon for replacement. He buys a lot of new underwear, socks, and shoes. He tells me everyone replaces these things at least once a year. Everyone that is but me.

If it's not uncomfortable, I can't part with it. I wore one pair of shoes for an entire year. "Last Gal Standing," the maker called them. Fabulous standing shoes. *All-day* standing shoes. So comfortable, I wore them until the soles wore out.

I kept my comfortable shoes until I could no longer wear them on rainy days. I finally had to admit, my leaky old shoes had to go. Even then, it wasn't easy. *Could I save them for sunny days?*

"You know," he continued, "We make too much money for you to walk around with holes in your clothes."

I suppose he's right. But I no longer shop to soothe my ego or buy new shoes because there's a sale. I won't spend $5 for an item I don't love but might forsake half a paycheck on a super comfy piece. I'm paying for longevity and comfort.

Clothes need not only "feel good," I must need them. It's not that I can't afford to buy them, but I want to see my money used elsewhere most of the time.

Experience shows me that the latter decades of our life open our eyes to seeing material things as temporary. Human comfort is short-lived and always beckoning to be replaced by something better. I've discovered these "comforts" don't last, and no matter how many temporal things we gain, things do not satisfy us. We want more. Why? Things are transitional. They never fill us. We long for something bigger.

They plaster tabloids with proof that riches don't make people happy. Often the poor are most grateful and satisfied. Even I recall with joy, leaner, carefree days when life seemed less complicated.

I believe everyone comes to a place when they step outside themselves and realize the simple, happy-go-lucky days brought comfort. Moments make a happy life. Glimpses of heaven, God allows us to enjoy where material things don't matter. A good life is God-centered, not possession-focused.

The world says whatever makes us uncomfortable, say goodbye. We stay in relationships while they're comfortable. If they aren't suitable, we're still willing to wait it out. If it's comfortable. Will it improve, or not? Then something offends us, and we're no longer comfortable. Courage gives us permission to toss out the old and bring on the new. Discomfort wins.

Recalling the conversation about my holes opened my eyes to see that God revealed He doesn't look at our holes. Just like we are with our own children, God looks past his children's imperfections, and he works on pruning and preparing them for his timing.

I am grateful that Jesus never leaves us or forsakes us when our actions become offensive and uncomfortable. We're more like the old shirt he continues to keep, no matter what. Undoubtedly, countless times in a day, we are offensive to someone, falling short of who we claim to be. Promise after promise, we say what we will do and don't. We get comfortable *being* uncomfortable *with* others.

Yet, full of holes, the potter knows precisely how he plans to use us. He sees our potential even when we don't. He takes our mess and molds us into something beautiful. He erases our hurts and smooths out our rough edges. His love fills the holes in our hearts and soul. God is our purest form of comfort.

I am a holey shirt. Flawed and broken.

We can change our clothes, but the shirt that covers us eventually wears out, and our real nature surfaces to reveal that no matter how far we've come, there's still a lot of work to be done. Despite our greatest efforts to restore ourselves, we are powerless until the Almighty has His way with us.

Our Father continues to love us and fill the crevices of our hearts, making us brand new. Each day, glory to glory.

He Speaks Enduring Love

God's love is so much different from the love the world offers. Human love has all kinds of strings attached. It says we will be loved if we are loveable. If we act a certain way and do the right things. It's conditional.

God's love is not based on emotions. He doesn't love us more if we are good, and He won't love us less if we fail to worship Him. God IS love! (1John 4:8)

Humans love people that love them. God loves us first.

Psalm 136 reminds us that God's love continues forever. Think about that. Forever. No matter what we do, no matter how far we stray, His love does not change. We may have caused consequences that aren't pleasant, but God's love hasn't changed. God never cannot fulfill His promises to us.

Unlike our family and friends who may not have patience for our moods and actions, God will forgive our sins and He does it with unconditional love, meaning he will forgive and forget. He will remember our sins no more.

"The Lord, your God, is in your midst, a mighty one who will save; He will rejoice over you with gladness; He will quiet you by His love; He will exult over you with loud singing.

Zephaniah 3:17

Prayer

Father, thank you for loving me. When I think about how I love other people and see how You love me in return, I am humbled. Who am I that you should care for me so profoundly? Amid my flaws, you love me as a treasure. Help mold me so I can love more like You do.

In Jesus' name. Amen.

REFLECTION

Recall and write about a time you have felt the sting of criticism?

_____

_____

_____

_____

How has criticism from others impacted the way you have felt God's thoughts about you?

_____

_____

_____

_____

Think about a time a situation was uncomfortable, and you stayed. What happened?

_____

_____

_____

_____

Describe the way our heavenly Father loves us differently than the love we receive from others?

_____

_____

_____

_____

_____

_____

_____

_____

_____

_____

_____

_____

_____

_____

_____

_____

_____

_____

Journal Your Story

HE SPOKE

127

CHAPTER 9

Pressed Down & Shaken

It had been a few weeks since we visited Pat. A lively Brooklyn native replanted in Virginia decades before, although she still had a strong New York dialect. There wasn't a drop of southern immersion in her. Probably because, in her mind, she had never left.

As a fellow New Yorker, I felt an instant connection to her. I longed to hear her stories of the big city I had lived so close to but never experienced. I fantasized about the excitement, glamour, and glitz of Manhattan and Times Square. But it was also a place with a dark side one could get lost in. For me, New York City seemed like a battle zone in another world compared to the serene countryside I grew up in, in upstate New York. So, I never went but wanted to. And it was almost like I did, living vicariously through the stories of Pat. The first thing I said to her at every visit was, "Tell me about what you loved most about New York City."

"I luvd the little cahs!" she would tell us of Coney Island as she rocked her arms back and forth as she pretended to drive.

Pat was a tiny woman of under 5 feet. So adorable you couldn't resist hugging her. I imagined her as a sprite young woman frolicking with her girlfriends on the boardwalk of Coney Island on a sizzling summer day.

"Ohw, I remember it as if it was yestaday," she would say in her dialect.

She told us that her father was a Police Officer, and he was busy "checking out the place" to make sure it was free of villains and weak floorboards, she would say as she tested the floor. She assured us we were in excellent hands. We replied that we all appreciated that. Then, she would tell us about her Swedish mother, who loved to cook and had an enormous meal ready. Her father would pick her up soon.

So, we waited with her until we had to leave and told her that her father would likely be there any minute. She was sad to see us go, but eager to see her father. The routine was the same week, but it engrossed us in her stories as she recanted them again with the same enthusiasm as the week before. Detail upon detail, nothing changed. And each week, we applauded and asked for more.

Our chance meeting with Pat and a few of the others in this community came when we had our own struggles. I was a single mom enduring a difficult phase without a job, so day to day became a challenge. I prayed but am ashamed to say I worried most of the time. Then I felt God speak to my heart and say, stop worrying about all your troubles and get out and meet a few of my children with genuine problems.

That's when my daughter and I found ourselves at a senior nursing home and rehabilitation center. Soon we had met a dozen residents who warmed up to us and delighted in our visits. We would stroll through the facility going door to door, visiting complete strangers who recognized us each week and seemed eager to see us.

What started as a weekly visit on Sunday afternoon soon became a ritual, expanding to include weekday and nighttime stays. We were addicted, but more than that, we were falling in love with these people who had become our family. We learned about their lives, hopes, and dreams. Many had no family. We had no family in the state, so these beautiful people were quickly etched into our hearts.

We chatted with them in their rooms, took them for walks, wheeled them around the facility, painted their nails, read to them, and even played dominoes until the late hours of the night. Going to the nursing home was something we looked forward to.

Suddenly, it wasn't at all that we were trying to do anything for them. They were our friends, and we were eager to see them. This eclectic group of residents brought more joy into our lives than we could have possibly given them. Giving came back to us triple, pressed down, shaken over, and more than we could imagine.

He Speaks to Comfort Us

We all need encouragement. Sometimes we can encourage ourselves, but other times we need more. When we are on the verge of giving up, remember that God will only give us what we can handle. Charles Stanley says, "The dark moments of our life will last only so long as is necessary for God to accomplish His purpose in me."

If you are living in a cloudy phase of life, don't lose hope. God will speak comfort in your life even during these times. Sometimes it's what we do in the dark that will bless us the most. Our blessings are shared. God doesn't give us what we have for ourselves. He gives it so we can give it away to be a blessing to somebody experiencing a dark moment.

Maya Angelou once said that we should be a rainbow in somebody else's cloud. I've learned that even if we have clouds in our own life, we can still be a rainbow in someone else's life. The more rainbows we make in other people's lives, the more light appears over our own clouds, if not making them disappear altogether.

The purpose in the dark time might be that God wants us to see we aren't alone. That He is with us and ready to get us through, even if He must carry us. And maybe that's when we can best carry someone else.

"And let ours also learn to maintain good works for necessary uses, that they may be not unfruitful."

Philemon 3:14

Prayer

Father, nothing we do to help others is a waste. Help me remember that when I am hurting, someone is hurting more. When I am lonely, someone is more lonesome. Give me the grace to put others before myself that my good toward them will develop fruit. I am convinced what I give to others comes back.

In Jesus' name. Amen.

REFLECTION

Recall a time when you felt helpless. How did you get through the tough time?

_____

_____

_____

_____

_____

_____

In what ways can you give to those that God has placed in your life?

_____

_____

_____

_____

_____

_____

_____

_____

Recall a time you were given an unexpected blessing.

_____

_____

_____

_____

_____

_____

_____

How could you be a rainbow in someone's cloud today?

_____

_____

_____

_____

_____

_____

_____

_____

_____

_____

JOURNAL YOUR STORY

HE SPOKE

EPILOGUE

Life's journey will take you through many seasons, bringing with it a mix of joy and sadness, challenges, and times of celebration. No trip is more important than your spiritual journey.

God promises to lead and give us abundant life. He instructs us how to have that best experience here on earth and prepare for eternal life. It's all freely offered, and all we must do is accept this gift.

If you have not allowed God to be the navigator of your life, I encourage you to place your trust in him. The Lord promises that if we draw near to him, he will draw near to us. He is as close as we want him to be.

As you walk with the Almighty, you will grow more rooted in faith, and your awareness of God's blessings will surround you. You'll have peace you can't understand and strength in your weakest moments. Life isn't always comfortable, but in him, the yoke is light. There will be peace in the storm. Jesus gives us the perseverance to press on and overcome challenges.

If you have never placed your trust in Jesus, I invite you to read the Roman Road. God has a plan for your life, and he's ready to reveal it if you let him. Call on him with a sincere heart, and he will listen and embrace you with open arms.

The Roman Road

"As it is written, there is no one righteous, not even one."

Romans 3:10 KJV

"For all have sinned and fall short of the glory of God."

Romans 3:23 KJV

"For the wages of sin is death, but the gift of God is eternal life through Jesus Christ our Lord.

Romans 6:23 KJV

"But God commended his love toward us in that, while we were yet sinners, Christ died for us.

Romans 5:8 KJV

"That if thou shalt confess with thy mouth the Lord Jesus, and shalt believe in thine heart that God has raised Him from the dead, thou shalt be saved.

Romans 10:9 KJV

"For with the heart man believeth unto righteousness, and with the mouth, confession is made unto salvation."

Romans 10:10 KJV

"For whosoever shall call on the name of the Lord shall be saved."

Romans 10:13 KJV

ABOUT THE AUTHOR

DIANA LÉGERE is a Christian writer whose passion is to share her faith and life experiences through her words, and help other women do the same.

As the founder of the Christian women's coaching, Faith Writer's Bridge, she works with first-time authors to provide editing, ghostwriting, and publishing services to help new authors get their words in print.

She is the author of four books, including the cookbook *Feeding Families Authentic Southern: Recipes, Traditions & Stories*, the memoir journal *Ripples: A Memoir of Reflection*, and *Celebrations of Praise: 365 Ways to Fill Each Day with Meaningful Moments*, and most recent, He Spoke, A Memoir of Grace.

A regular contributor to Crosswalk, she has also written for Propel, and Christian Parenting, and many regional magazines and newspapers.

A New York native, Diana now lives in central Virginia. A mother of three and a grandmother of two, she's as happy on the road (five cross-country road trips and counting) as she is with a green tea on the couch binge-watching an entire season of I Love Lucy. Besides her writing, she loves painting, music, photography, and her little chihuahua, Pablo.

BOOKS BY DIANA

He Spoke
A Memoir of Grace

Celebrations of Praise
365 Ways to Fill Each Day with Meaningful Moments

Ripples
A Memoir of Reflection

Authentic Southern
Recipes, Traditions & Stories

CPSIA information can be obtained
at www.ICGtesting.com
Printed in the USA
LVHW040150050522
717841LV00053B/2717

9 780997 912616